A Variety Book of Puppet Scripts

Sarah Walton Miller

Broadman Press
Nashville, Tennessee

4275-15
ISBN: 0-8054-7515-X

Dewey Decimal Classification: 812
Subject heading: PUPPETS AND PUPPET PLAYS

Library of Congress Catalog Card Number: 78-057276
Printed in the United States of America

Introduction

This book contains puppet scripts for use at various times in the church. Seven are meant for parties or fellowship times. Others are intended for classes or study groups to spark discussion. Some points for discussion are suggested. Add others. The suggested age group is indicated with the title of each skit in the table of contents; some are for children but the majority are for youth and adults.

It is not necessary to purchase puppets. The cost may prevent the purchase of enough puppets for the presentations. Instead, try making puppets from inexpensive materials such as socks, Styrofoam balls, cloth, paper, and papier–mâche. They will fit your needs more accurately and will allow you as many puppets as you need.

Three books which will give new puppeteers help in making and using hand puppets are:

Be a Puppeteer by Estelle Worrell, published by McGraw-Hill Book Co., New York City.

Puppet Making Through the Grades by Grizella Hopper, published by Davis Publications Inc., Worcester, Mass.

Using Puppetry in the Church, edited by Everett Robertson, published by Convention Press, Nashville, Tenn.

Other puppet skits may be found in *Puppet Scripts for Use at Church,* edited by Everett Robertson and obtainable from Church Services and Materials Division, 127 Ninth Avenue North, Nashville, Tenn. 37234.

Contents

Discussion Skits

Fellowships and Parties

1. Stealing?

Four puppets: MOTHER, FATHER, DAUGHTER, SON

(MOTHER *and* FATHER *are reading the paper.*)

MOTHER: Did you have a good day?

FATHER: So-so.

MOTHER: The bill came from the Mercantile and guess what!

FATHER: I can't guess. Tell me.

MOTHER *(gleefully):* They forgot to charge us with the gown I bought for Aunt Bessie's birthday!

(SON *and* DAUGHTER *enter.*)

DAUGHTER *(shouting):* I'm going to tell on you!

SON *(shouting):* I don't care if you do! Tattletale, tattletale!

FATHER: Here, here. What's the matter?

DAUGHTER: Daddy, Bobby found Jessica's fifty cents and isn't going to tell her!

SON: Well, she shouldn't be so careless.

DAUGHTER: That's *stealing!*

SON: No, it isn't! I didn't take it. I just *found* it.

DAUGHTER *(shouting):* Yes, but you know she's been looking everywhere for it! It *is* stealing, isn't it, Daddy?

SON: Mom, make her leave me alone.

MOTHER: Well, Son, if you know whose money it is, don't you think you'll feel better giving it back?

FATHER: Eleanor, it isn't a matter of *feeling* better. It's a matter of right and wrong.

DAUGHTER *(shouting):* See? I told you it was stealing!

SON *(shouting):* It is not! When you find something just laying there, that's *finding*, not stealing. Tell her I'm right, Dad.

FATHER: It seems to me you are forgetting Jessica. Won't she miss her fifty cents? Won't Jessica feel badly?

SON: Oh, who cares. Jessica is a pill anyway.

DAUGHTER: She doesn't like you either!

MOTHER: Your father is right. You must give it back, Son. The fifty cents belongs to Jessica and to keep it *is* stealing. So give it back.

SON: Oh, rats!

DAUGHTER: See? I told you so!

SON *(starts toward her):* I'll get even with you!

DAUGHTER: Motherrrr! Make him leave me alone!

MOTHER: Son!

SON: Aw—all right.

(SON *and* DAUGHTER *leave.*)

MOTHER: It's hard to teach children right and wrong these days, what with all that goes on around them.

FATHER: About that bill from the Mercantile . . .

MOTHER *(happily):* Yes, wasn't that lucky? Just like a Christmas present?

(MOTHER *and* FATHER *leave.*)

For Discussion

1. What were the "wrongs" committed in this skit?
2. Are they true to life?
3. What is the *real* trouble here?

8

2. The Judgment

Puppets: JUDGE, BAILIFF, MRS. MORGAN, MRS. HENDRICKS, DOG
  Prop: Judge's bench or table

(JUDGE *enters behind bench.*)

JUDGE: Bailiff, bring in the first case.

(BAILIFF *enters with two women and a dog. Throughout, the dog reacts with whines and woofs.*)

BAILIFF: Your Honor, *Morgan versus Hendricks.*

JUDGE: What is the complaint?

MORGAN: *Complaint?* Your judgeship, this woman stole my dog! *(in honeyed tones to dog)* Didn't she, Snookems?

HENDRICKS: *Snookems!* That dog's name is *Rover,* and he's mine!

(MORGAN *and* HENDRICKS *ad lib several "he is!" and "he isn't!".*)

JUDGE: Silence! Bailiff, if either of these women makes any more disturbance, escort her out of the courtroom!

BAILIFF: Yes, your Honor.

JUDGE: Now that you have settled down, suppose you tell me your side of the case, Mrs. Morgan.

MORGAN: Your judgeship—

JUDGE *(correcting her):* Your Honor.

MORGAN *(surprised:)* I'm not an Honor! I'm just a Mrs.!

JUDGE *(patiently):* Never mind. Go on.

MORGAN: I had Snookems out in the front yard playing with a ball—

HENDRICKS: The ball was too small, your Honor! Rover could have choked on it!

MORGAN *(loudly):* Snookems is a sensible dog! Well, anyway, there we were. Then *she* came down the street.

JUDGE: Did you know her?

MORGAN: She lives about two blocks up the street, but I never saw her before.

HENDRICKS *(angrily):* Except when I came by last month asking if you had seen my dog, Rover!

MORGAN: You didn't!

(MORGAN *and* HENDRICKS *"you did" and "you didn't" until stopped by the* BAILIFF.)

BAILIFF: Here, here! Quiet down or out you go! Settle down now.

JUDGE: Go on.

MORGAN: Well, she started yelling—

HENDRICKS: I yelled, "Thief! Thief!" because that's what she is!

JUDGE: Mrs. Hendricks, please wait your turn. Go on, Mrs. Morgan.

MORGAN: Well, she grabbed Snookems and I grabbed him, too, and then the police came. They said we had to come here.

JUDGE: Now, Mrs. Hendricks, what have you to say?

HENDRICKS: Rover is my dog, your Honor. He disappeared from my yard about a month ago. I advertised for him, and I went all over the neighborhood to see if anyone had seen him. I *did* go by her house, and she said she hadn't seen him! All the time she had him shut up somewhere!

MORGAN: That's a lie! I did no such thing!

JUDGE: How long have you had this dog, Mrs. Morgan?

MORGAN: A long time. Ever since he was a tiny puppy!

JUDGE: How long?

MORGAN: About—about two years.

HENDRICKS: There! Now you know she's lying! Rover is five years old. Any good vet can tell you his age.

MORGAN: Don't believe her, your judgeship!

JUDGE *(correcting her):* Your Honor.

MORGAN: Huh?

JUDGE: Never mind. Now, Mrs. Morgan, you say the dog is yours?

MORGAN: My Snookems!

JUDGE: Mrs. Hendricks, you say the dog is yours.

HENDRICKS: Rover *is* my dog!

JUDGE: Well, there's no fair way to decide this case unless . . . Bailiff!

BAILIFF: Yes, your Honor?

JUDGE: Take Snookems-Rover to the veterinarian. Have him cut into two equal pieces and give half to each woman.

BAILIFF: Yes, Sir. Here, dog!

HENDRICKS: Oh, no!

MORGAN: Go ahead! I'd rather he died than give him to her!

HENDRICKS: Wait! Your Honor, don't punish Rover for our human faults. I'll let her have him.

JUDGE: That decides it. Mrs. Hendricks, the dog is yours. The true owner would think of the dog first.

HENDRICKS: Oh, thank you, your Honor! Come, Rover!

(HENDRICKS exits with DOG, who barks and whines joyfully.)

JUDGE: Mrs. Morgan, I order you to pay court costs and a fifty-dollar fine for stealing the dog.

MORGAN: I didn't steal him! He just came to my house by himself. Probably wasn't happy with *her!*

JUDGE: Nevertheless, by concealing him, you broke the law. Bailiff, escort her out.

(BAILIFF *shows* MORGAN *to exit and returns.*)

BAILIFF: All done. No more cases today. Your Honor, this case reminds me of something I heard somewhere. Can't quite place it though. Must have been another case in this court.

JUDGE: Not this court. Another court a long time ago.

(JUDGE *and* BAILIFF *leave.*)

3. The Cheat

Puppets: PETE, JOE, and HARRIET

PETE *(angrily):* You shouldn't have done it!

JOE *(lightly):* Aw, come on, Pete. Why the holier-than-thou pose? You cheat sometimes. Besides I'm your friend.

PETE: This is different! Don't try to crawfish out of it! I can get along without friends like you!

(HARRIET *enters.*)

HARRIET: Boys! Boys! What's the argument?

PETE: Harriet, *you* tell Joe!

HARRIET: Tell Joe what?

PETE: It's wrong to cheat. Cheating is stealing!

JOE: Aw, Pete's all steamed up because I copied his *last* year's term theme. Miss Davis wasn't his teacher so she'll never know.

PETE: That was *my* paper, *my* brains, and *my* work!

JOE: Well, I thought you wouldn't mind giving a hand to an old friend.

HARRIET: Pete is right, Joe. That was wrong for you to do.

JOE: I told you I didn't have time to do my own.

PETE: Why not? You had as much time as everyone else.

HARRIET: Pete's right. Listen, Joe. Why do you think teachers assign these term papers?

JOE: To complicate my life?

HARRIET: Joe!

JOE: Because they hate us?

HARRIET: Don't joke! These assignments teach us to think and to search out ideas. Pete did all the thinking on what you turned in.

JOE *(ruefully):* Yeah, I guess.

HARRIET: *You* didn't learn a thing. Besides cheating Pete, you cheated yourself of the learning. Do you see?

JOE *(ruefully):* I guess so.

PETE *(relenting):* Aw, let it go.

HARRIET *(sternly):* No, Pete. This is a matter of Joe's character. When he cheated, he stole your ideas. It's a sin to steal.

PETE: Aw, Harriet—

HARRIET: Pete! Don't back off now. Joe will thank you for being firm. The only way to build character is to be honest. Do your own work. Am I right, Joe?

JOE: Yes, you are. Pete, I'm sorry. I promise never to steal your ideas again. Will you forgive me?

PETE: Of course. Forget it.

HARRIET: I'm glad you two are making up. Friends again?

PETE: Friends again. Thanks, Harriet.

HARRIET: Don't mention it. Well, I've got some shopping to do. Good-bye.

(HARRIET *starts off, then stops.*)

PETE and JOE: 'Bye, Harriet.

13

(HARRIET *turns back.*)

HARRIET *(sternly):* By the way, the other day when we all went swimming, somebody stole my Holiday Inn towel, and I want it back!

(HARRIET *leaves.* PETE *and* JOE *look at each other, then leave.*)

For Discussion

1. Cheating is common. Does that make it right?
2. Do we often criticize the failings of others and ignore our own? Comment.

4. Honesty

Two puppets

ONE: Come over to my house and I'll show you my collection of embroidered towels.

TWO *(surprised):* Embroidered towels?

ONE *(snickering):* Yeah. Embroidered with "Holiday Inn," "Ramada," "Hilton," "Sheraton"—

TWO: You mean you *took* their towels?

ONE: Why not? They got plenty.

TWO: But that's not honest!

ONE *(indignantly):* Look who's talking! Of course it's honest.

TWO: You don't know what honest is.

ONE: Sure I do. Honest is when you tell your neighbor who you saw run over his new garbage can.

TWO: No, it isn't. Honesty is not taking what you don't pay for.

14

ONE: If you mean those towels—I paid for them and don't you forget it! Have you stayed in a hotel or motel lately?

TWO: It's still not honest to take things from the room.

ONE: Oh, go fly a kite!

TWO: Just because they left the towels *there* didn't mean you were to take them. I bet if you were going along the street and saw a broken shop window, you'd take something!

ONE: Like what?

TWO: Anything. A toaster, for instance.

ONE: You mean—it's just there in plain sight? Anyone could pick it up?

TWO: Yes.

ONE: Well, sure I'd take it. I could use a new toaster; besides, if I didn't take it, someone else would.

TWO: But that's *dishonest!*

ONE: No, it isn't. In a way, it's a lesson to the shopkeeper. He ought to be more careful.

TWO *(disgusted):* I'll bet if you got that toaster home and it didn't work, you'd send it back to the factory for *free repairs!*

ONE *(shocked):* No, I wouldn't! The toaster didn't cost *me* anything! To make the factory fix it for nothing would be dishonest! What do you think I am?

TWO *(leaving):* Aw, I give up!

(They both leave.)

For Discussion

1. What is your definition of *honesty?*
2. Have you ever taken something that didn't belong to you? Would you do it again?
3. Does honesty extend beyond physical things? For example, does fibbing or lying enter in? What about leaving false impressions?

4. Is it *easier* to be honest or dishonest? Always?
5. Do you admire honesty in a person? Why?

5. Sidetracked

Two puppets

ONE: Yoohoo! YOOHOO! *YOOHOO!*

TWO: I hear you. They probably hear you downtown.

ONE: Then why didn't you answer?

TWO: I didn't know you meant me.

ONE: Who do you see around here but us?

TWO: Nobody, I guess.

ONE: Then couldn't you figure I meant you?

TWO: It wasn't up to me to figure. It was up to you to call my name.

ONE: *(hotly):* That's belaboring the point!

TWO: What?

ONE: Belaboring! BELABORING! Oh, use your common sense!

TWO: Statistics show that common sense is very uncommon.

ONE: I believe it! But try, anyway!

TWO: I think of myself as average.

ONE: Don't overestimate.

TWO: Well, if we're going to end up by calling names, maybe we'd better stop this conversation.

ONE: It's okay by me.

TWO: What did you want?

ONE: Want?

TWO: When you were yelling "yoohoo."

(ONE *looks about thoughtfully, doing something physical if possible, as scratching his head.*)

ONE: Uh—uh—I forget!

TWO: You *forget?* After all this hassle?

ONE: It was the hassle that made me forget! It's all your fault! Good-bye!

(ONE *leaves. After a pause,* TWO *speaks.*)

TWO: I guess the moral is— don't be sidetracked from the main issue, no matter how you are tempted. Stick to the main truth, no matter what.

(TWO *leaves.*)

For Discussion

1. Is it difficult to pick out the main truth in a lesson or the main issue in life?
2. Do we give enough serious thought to our own goals?

6. People-Watching

Two puppets

ONE: I always wanted to be an angel sitting on a cloud.

TWO: Why?

ONE: To look down and see what people are doing.

TWO: Help yourself. Look around you now. Those are people.

ONE: Not like this! They can see me watching them. They couldn't see an angel. I'm no angel.

TWO: Agreed.

ONE: Up on a cloud I could see everywhere. And if I were an angel, no one could see me.

TWO: Why do you care if they see you? Why does it matter?

ONE: People don't act the same if they think someone is watching them. It's a fascinating idea and would be a lot of fun.

TWO: Fun?

ONE: Think what I could have seen in the past. Imagine *watching* history instead of reading about it. Suppose a long time ago I was up on my cloud and I could see Jonah down there in the streets of Nineveh!

TWO *(leaning over as if looking down into Nineveh)*: What's he doing?

ONE: He's preaching on the corner. See? People are gathering around. Listen to him shout!

TWO *(as if quoting, in a high, far-away voice)*: "Unless you repent, you will all die. . . ." *(normal voice)* I say! They are laughing at him!

ONE: Not all of them. Look at those three over by the bakery shop.

TWO *(with pity)*: Poor Jonah! He's discouraged. See, he's turning away. They are jeering at him!

ONE: Not the three by the bakery shop. Look at them.

TWO *(surprised)*: Yes, I see. Why, they are taking him seriously!

ONE: Those are the people who listen and believe and go tell the king. He makes everyone listen. So the city is saved.

TWO *(after a pause)*: All that from a seat on a cloud?

ONE: No. From the Bible.

TWO: Then the Bible is like a seat on a cloud. With a Bible, you can look in on a lot of people's lives!

ONE: I suppose.

TWO: Well, one thing's sure.

ONE: What?

TWO: You're still no angel!

(They leave.)

For Discussion

1. Do you ever watch people and wonder about them?
2. Are you critical of what you see without attempting to understand why people acted as they did?
3. Is it hard for most people to communicate with others?
4. Knowing what kind of person you are and what motivates *you*—if *you* had been a Ninevite and had seen this ragged preacher on a corner shouting out a doomsday message, what might *you* have done?
5. Is anyone shouting now to deaf ears in this company?

7. The Talk Show

Puppets: the Talk Show HOST, NOAH, SHEM (Noah's son)
Props: taped "theme" music; sign—"The Afternoon Show"
Sign covers stage opening. When it is removed, the three puppets are seen.

HOST: Good afternoon, ladies and gentlemen. This is Merv Stone, your host, welcoming you to this edition of The Afternoon Show. Today our guests are Noah and his son Shem. Mr. Noah, since some of our viewers may not know who you are, let's start by reminding them of recent headlines. It seems you are building an unusual boat.

NOAH: That's true.

HOST: A rather large boat.

NOAH: 450 feet long, 75 feet wide, and 45 feet high. Three stories in all.

HOST: In a boat, that's "decks."

NOAH: Whatever.

HOST: This boat is sitting out there on the edge of the desert?

NOAH: Right now it is.

HOST: Is there a river or lake nearby?

NOAH: No.

HOST: Then how do you plan to float such a boat?

NOAH: *I* don't.

HOST: So you're building a boat you don't expect to be able to float?

SHEM: Now my dad didn't say that—exactly.

HOST: Shem, are you helping your father build this boat?

SHEM: My brothers and I.

HOST: Your brothers didn't come with you, I see.

SHEM: They're off leading in the animals while Dad and I finish the boat. Mom and our wives are getting food in for the animals.

HOST *(surprised):* Do I understand you plan to put *animals* in this huge boat that won't ever go anywhere?

SHEM *(enthusiastically): Lots* of them! Two of every kind on earth!

HOST: *Two* of . . . . Are you *serious?* This is for *real?*

SHEM: Oh it's for real, all right. And a lot of hard work.

HOST: Uh—I see. Now, Noah, you won't be offended, will you, if I say I find this whole enterprise unbelievable?

NOAH: No, Son. Can't say I blame you much. When I first told the boys and the women what I had in mind, you should have

20

heard *them!* But they came around, didn't you, Shem?

SHEM: Right on, Dad!

HOST: Where did you get the idea?

NOAH: Well, I was out talking to the Lord, and *he* told me to get that boat ready. He said to bring two of every animal on earth into the boat.

HOST: The "Lord"?

NOAH: *God.* Do you know our God?

HOST *(embarrassed):* Uh—well—I've heard of many gods—

NOAH: No, no! Not those trashy statues. My God is the God of the universe. Mi-i-ighty big!

HOST *(nervously):* So he sounds.

NOAH: So when *he* says jump, I *jump!*

SHEM: Dad, we'd better be going. Not much time left.

NOAH: That's right. Well, Son, it's been nice meeting you. Too bad it won't last.

HOST: I don't understand.

NOAH: Son, there's gonna be rain like you never saw before.

SHEM: Like *nobody* ever saw before!

HOST: Out here? Why our annual rainfall seldom reaches twelve inches.

NOAH: Well, this time it's going twelve *feet* and twelve feet more and as many more times twelve as God needs to wash his earth clean again. Come, Shem.

(NOAH *and* SHEM *leave. Theme music starts.)*

HOST: There you have it, folk. If you'd be interested in driving out to see this monstrosity next Sunday or the Sunday after, take the highway east for about fifteen miles. You can't miss it. This is your Afternoon Show host, Merv Stone, saying goodbye with a word of advice. If you go out there Sunday, take

21

an umbrella. It'll keep the *sun* off! *(laughs)*

(Sign covers front. HOST *leaves. Music stops. Remove sign.)*

For Discussion

1. In the midst of prosperity, is it difficult to preach that hard times are coming?
2. Do people tend to face spiritual needs when things are going well for them?
3. Should warnings not be given just because people won't listen?

8. Faith

Two puppets

ONE: Faith is the substance of things hoped for, the evidence of things not seen.

TWO *(not really caring):* What does *that* mean?

ONE: Faith is something you have in what you can't see or touch.

TWO: Who said so?

ONE: God did.

TWO *(scoffing):* What does *he* know!

ONE: He invented it.

TWO: For people only. Not for him. He doesn't need faith. He knows everything. So he doesn't have to have faith.

ONE: How about when he sent Jesus?

TWO: He knew what would happen. That's not faith.

ONE: Yes, but he had to have faith that the people Jesus left would *do* something. Now what do you say to that?

TWO: He knew they would!

ONE: Sure, but they had a choice. He had faith because he knew how they'd think and act.

TWO: That's what I said.

ONE: No, you didn't. You meant they moved at *God's* choice, not their own. But that's not so. God had faith because he *knew them*. See?

TWO: No.

ONE: Well, I have faith, but it's not based on stupidity. I know God. I know Jesus. Therefore I have faith based on knowledge. Now do you understand?

TWO: Oh, never mind! It's not important that I understand.

ONE: On the contrary. It's the most important thing in your life.

(They leave.)

For Discussion

Is it difficult to make your unbelieving friends understand what you mean by *faith?*

9. Let's Trade

Two puppets

ONE: Hi! Where you going?

TWO *(groans):* Just *away!*

ONE: Away? Away where?

TWO: Anywhere but here.

ONE: What's the matter with here?

23

TWO: My *brother!*

ONE: Your brother? What's with your brother?

TWO: In this whole country no one has a worse brother than I have.

ONE: Oh, no! You don't know *my* brother.

TWO: Yours couldn't be the pest mine is. He drives me wild. Sometimes I can't stand it.

ONE: Yeah, I know how you feel. There ought to be a law against brothers like that. No one's brother is a worst pest than mine.

TWO: Oh, no? What I could tell you about mine! Sheer poison. That's what he is.

ONE: Say, I have an idea. Why don't we swap brothers?

TWO: You mean—trade brothers?

ONE: Yeah! I couldn't possibly do worse.

TWO: I don't see how I could either.

ONE: A deal?

TWO: A deal!

ONE: Well, now that's settled, what's new?

(TWO *is silent for a long pause.* ONE *waits and finally speaks again.)*

ONE: Did you hear me? I said . . . .

TWO: I heard.

ONE: Well?

TWO: I'm still thinking about—well, about my brother.

ONE: He's not your brother now. He's mine.

TWO: Yeah, but—well . . . .

ONE: Are you trying to get out of our deal?

TWO: Oh, no! I'm just—thinking of my mother. She kinda likes him.

24

ONE: She does? Why?

TWO: I don't know. Something, I guess.

ONE *(hopefully):* Maybe there's more to him than you think.

TWO: Oh, I don't know. Anyway—well—

ONE *(graciously):* OK, you can have him back.

TWO: Thanks! I'll go tell him he's still my brother. 'Bye. (TWO *leaves.)*

ONE: I'd rather keep my own brother too. But I didn't want *him* to know that. I had to help him somehow. Poor guy! He really *does* have the worst brother in the world!

(ONE *leaves.)*

For Discussion

1. Do you quarrel with your brother or sister? Why?
2. Think of something good about him or her.
3. Have you tried imagining how *you* seem to him or her?
4. If someone tried to hurt your brother or sister, what would you do?

10. The Commitment

Puppets: LUTIE, a female; ELMER, carrying a pledge card and wearing a hat with a band around it saying, "Pledge Now"; FLASH, a male wearing gaudy rags, wild hair, and dirt.

(ELMER *enters, looks around.* LUTIE *enters.)*

ELMER: Hi, Lutie! I been looking for you.

LUTIE: Oh. My goodness, why are you wearing that funny hat?

ELMER: Aw, it's just an idea to get people to pledge the budget.

LUTIE *(annoyed):* Oh, dear! That again?

(FLASH *enters.*)

FLASH *(boisterously):* Hi, Man! Hi, Man! Hey, El, remember me?

ELMER *(not liking his appearance):* Uh—no . . . . Wait . . . You can't be—?

FLASH: Flash! Your old schoolmate in the eighth grade! Remember how I used to go home with you after school? Say, how's your mother?

ELMER *(coldly):* She's fine.

FLASH *(boisterously):* Remember how she used to take me to your Sunday School sometimes?

ELMER *(coldly):* I remember. That was a long time ago.

LUTIE *(makes a sound of disgust):* Ugh!

FLASH *(cheerfully):* You were saying something, Babe?

LUTIE: Certainly not!

ELMER *(embarrassed):* Uh—Lutie, this is Flash—someone I used to know.

LUTIE *(turns away):* Hmph.

FLASH *(pleasantly):* And a couple of "hmphs" to you, too, Babe. Well, El, what's with you these days?

ELMER: Lutie and I go to the same church. I'm—I'm out getting pledges to the budget.

FLASH: Oh?

LUTIE *(impatiently):* Is that all you want, Elmer?

ELMER: I guess you want to go and do whatever you were going to do, don't you, Lutie? What *were* you doing?

LUTIE *(her first enthusiastic response):* I'm going shopping, Elmer. All these marvelous sales, you know. I've had my eye on some darling things. Now they are all marked down!

ELMER: How about signing your pledge card before you leave?

LUTIE *(annoyed)*: Not now, Elmer.

ELMER *(complaining)*: If I can give up my good time to come ask, the least people can do is sign!

LUTIE: Heavens, not me. I can't possibly decide what I'll give until I see how much I'll owe, can I?

FLASH: Well, pardon me, Princess—

LUTIE: Are you speaking to me?

FLASH: Yeah. Now, I'm not a churchgoer like you and old El, here, but aren't you guys supposed to *give* first and spend later?

LUTIE: Don't be silly. How would I have anything to spend if I gave it all away first?

ELMER *(plaintively)*: Just a tenth, Lutie? . . . or a twentieth?

LUTIE *(indignantly)*: A *twentieth!* A twentieth is two-tenths! Really, Elmer!

ELMER *(pleading)*: Well, something then? A dollar a week?

LUTIE: Now, Elmer, don't go nagging me. I'm sure I give as much as most people in the church. And if I don't, it's my own business. So there!

ELMER *(righteously)*: You should give a tenth. *I* do.

FLASH: That's telling her, Man!

LUTIE: You keep out of this, you—you—I'd just like to know how you have the nerve to criticize *me?*

ELMER: Now, Lutie—

LUTIE: You hush, Elmer! I'm going to say my say. Just look at him. I'll bet he doesn't have a job or a decent place to live or anything like *real* people have!

FLASH *(happily)*: Right, Babe!

LUTIE: You see? He doesn't even care!

FLASH *(happily)*: That makes me sort of like Jesus. Or so I heard.

27

LUTIE: Oh, you are impossible! How can you say such a disgusting thing?

ELMER: Lutie, hold your temper. Flash isn't a Christian like you and me.

FLASH: You can say that again, Man!

ELMER *(annoyed):* Now just a minute—

FLASH: No offense meant, El, old friend. No offense.

LUTIE: Just what *did* you mean by that remark?

FLASH: Aw—I don't want to start a ruckus.

LUTIE: I *said* what did you mean? Or are you afraid to explain yourself?

FLASH: Well, Babe, here goes. From where I'm sitting, as Christians, you and old El here aren't so much. How do you like that?

LUTIE *(angrily):* Ohhh! Elmer, are you going to stand there and let him say those things about me?

FLASH: Now, wait! You asked for it, Babe. I got a lot of respect for Jesus. But I can't say so much for some people who claim to follow him.

ELMER: Flash, you don't understand—

FLASH: No? You mean I don't go along with half measures. Oh, I know what you think of my way of life. But I'm honest about it. And that's more than you are.

LUTIE *(hysterically):* You are a horrid creature! You look like trash and you talk like trash and you are trash! Elmer, I'm going shopping and you can just wait until I'm good and ready for that old pledge card!

(LUTIE *leaves.*)

FLASH: I'm sorry I messed up your pitch, old man.

ELMER *(sighs):* Aw, that's okay. Lutie hardly ever signs a card anyway. She manages to squirm out of it nearly every time. The trouble with her is she has no real commitment.

FLASH *(curious):* Do you have a commitment?

ELMER: Certainly! I give a whole tenth. I am very careful to figure it out to the third decimal. No one can question my honesty.

FLASH: How about the rest of your money—the nine-tenths to the third decimal?

ELMER: That's mine! What do you mean?

FLASH: Oh, nothing. What do you do besides give a tenth?

ELMER: What do I *do?* Can't you *see?* Every year at this time, I go out and try to get people signed up. Especially people like Lutie who don't pledge. What do I *do?* What a question.

FLASH: That's all?

ELMER: Isn't that enough?

FLASH: All year long? What about the rest of the year?

ELMER: Money is important.

FLASH: Man, that's not much of a commitment. Just money.

ELMER: Look who's talking! You're not even a Christian.

FLASH: If I were a Christian, or anything else, I'd go all out for it!

ELMER *(sneering):* You probably *would,* with no restraint whatsoever. I'm sorry, Flash, but I've got things to do. See you around sometime.

(ELMER *leaves.)*

FLASH: Yeah, El, sometime. Hmm. I'd hate to be Jesus and have to depend on cats like El and that Lutie!

(FLASH *leaves.)*

For Discussion

1. What kind of commitment did Elmer and Lutie have?
2. Was Flash too hard on them?

3. Do people judge our church—and even Jesus—by our lives and attitudes? Or do they pay no attention to us at all?

11. The Runaway

Puppets: GRANDPA and JOHNNY

(GRANDPA *is sitting in a chair.* JOHNNY, *his grandson, enters. He doesn't say anything. After a silence,* GRANDPA *speaks.)*

GRANDPA: Well, you going to say good morning, Johnny?

JOHNNY *(glumly):* Good morning, Grandpa.

GRANDPA: Sound as if you got up on the wrong side of the bed. *(another long silence)* Want to talk about it, Johnny?

JOHNNY: Won't do any good!

GRANDPA: Oh, I don't know. Sometimes talking about it helps. Want to try me?

JOHNNY *(angrily):* If you have to know—I'm thinking of *running away!* Now I suppose you'll go tell Mom!

GRANDPA: Why?

JOHNNY: Because grown-ups all stick together.

GRANDPA: Is that how it looks to you?

JOHNNY: Yeah!

GRANDPA: Why are you thinking of running away?

JOHNNY: Because everything is a *mess!*

GRANDPA: Such as?

JOHNNY: I—I failed my algebra test.

GRANDPA: Well—I'd say that's serious. What happened? Algebra hasn't been hard for you before.

JOHNNY: Aw, I don't know.

GRANDPA: Did you study?

JOHNNY: Well—sure.

GRANDPA: I know you and your friends practice in that little band for hours every day.

JOHNNY: Aw, Grandpa!

GRANDPA: I always say if you study and do your best, your dead-level best with no alibiing—then if you fail, it's no big deal.

JOHNNY: I can't study all the time!

GRANDPA: That's true.

JOHNNY: Mom wants me to study all the time. She keeps asking me and asking me if I studied. I just can't please her! I can't do anything right!

GRANDPA: That's why you are thinking of running away?

JOHNNY: Yeah.

GRANDPA: I ran away once.

JOHNNY: You did?

GRANDPA: When I was about your age.

JOHNNY *(interested):* You *did?*

GRANDPA: It wasn't my mother. She died when I was five. It was my father who was after me.

JOHNNY: Did you fail algebra too?

GRANDPA: I failed the whole shebang. The whole grade.

JOHNNY: Didn't you study either?

GRANDPA: I *said* I did. But what I really did was mess around rebuilding a car I'd bought with money from mowing lawns that summer. A wrecked Model T. Cost me thirty dollars.

JOHNNY *(impressed):* Wow! You owned a Model T?

GRANDPA: Well, part of one. What wasn't smashed up. When I failed my grade, my father took it away and sent me to summer school all summer.

JOHNNY: All summer?

GRANDPA: To make up the lost grade.

JOHNNY: What did he do with the car?

GRANDPA: Stored it in my grandfather's barn out on the farm where I couldn't get at it.

JOHNNY: That wasn't fair! *You* paid for it!

GRANDPA: Well, my father said *his* job was to support us and pay a housekeeper to make a home for us, and *my* job was to get an education. And I wasn't doing my job. He said he'd remove temptation so I could study.

JOHNNY: So you ran away?

GRANDPA: Yep. Clear across the country. I thought he was unfair. If that was the way it was going to be, I didn't want any part of it.

JOHNNY: Did he come after you?

GRANDPA: No. After a week I came back.

JOHNNY: Why?

GRANDPA: Well, the only job I could get was washing dishes in a cheap cafe. Nobody else would hire me because I was too young and didn't have any education. I must have washed four million dishes! I slept on a cot in the storeroom and worked twelve to fourteen hours a day. At night I'd fall asleep before I could get into that cot! Was I ever tired! After a week of that, I had a new respect for what my father did. So I went home.

JOHNNY: What did he do to you?

GRANDPA: Oh, he didn't punish me if that's what you mean. He figured I'd had a hard enough time already, I suppose.

JOHNNY: Did you get the car back?

GRANDPA: When my grades were in and I passed, he gave the car back.

JOHNNY (rebelliously): I wouldn't have taken the old car!

GRANDPA: Why not? My father was right. *I'd* proved that. By then I felt I deserved the car. Yep, I fixed that car up and drove it for five years. Sold it for ten times what I'd paid for the wreck. Wish I had it now. Well, that's the only time I ever ran away. Now, here's you. When you planning to leave?

JOHNNY (grudgingly): Oh, I guess I didn't study so hard on that algebra.

GRANDPA: Oh? Going to give it another try?

JOHNNY: I guess . . . . Maybe the guys in the band can get along without me sometimes.

GRANDPA: Well, you have to make up your own mind. It's your decision.

JOHNNY: Yeah. Thanks, Grandpa, for listening.

(JOHNNY *Leaves.*)

GRANDPA (calls after him): Anytime, Johnny! Anytime!

(GRANDPA *leaves.*)

For Discussion

1. When things don't go right for us, are we honest in evaluating our own responsibility for the outcome?
2. Do we hunt for someone else to blame? Is it hard to admit we are wrong? Why?

12. Sign That Pledge Card!

Two puppets

ONE: Have you turned in your pledge card yet?

TWO: No, I threw it away.

ONE: You didn't!

TWO: Yes, I did.

ONE: Why did you do that?

TWO *(firmly):* Because I don't sign anything!

ONE: That's ridiculous.

TWO: Oh? Well, now, just suppose I signed it. Then in a couple of months I found I couldn't pay what I promised. The church would bill me and I'd be embarrassed.

ONE *(scoffing):* Of course they wouldn't! All you'd have to do is tell them you have to change your pledge.

TWO: Then they'd think I was a *failure.*

ONE: Anybody can run into bad luck. Besides, all God expects is a tithe of *whatever* you earn.

TWO: What's a tithe?

ONE: A tenth of your earnings.

TWO *(shocked):* A *tenth!* That's a lot!

ONE: The government takes more than that all the time and you don't kick.

TWO: Oh yes I do. But it doesn't get me anywhere. Oh, dear! I feel poor already. How much does the government take?

ONE: It varies. Maybe two tenths and more.

TWO *(alarmed):* That would be three tenths! I can't afford that!

ONE: Some people pay six tenths or more.

TWO: Then with all that why does the church need *my* tenth?

ONE: You've got it wrong. The church doesn't get the three or six tenths or whatever. The *government* does.

TWO: Then what does the church get?

ONE: One tenth.

TWO: Well, that's more like it! Not *three?*

ONE: God says one is enough. So you'll sign up for a tenth?

TWO: Now, I didn't say that.

ONE: But you have to sign!

TWO: Why? The church has a tenth and that's what you said was enough?

ONE: It doesn't *have* a tenth until you sign up and give it!

TWO: But that's not what you said. You said the government got two or three or six or whatever tenths, while the church got one.

ONE *(exasperated):* Under the circumstances you'd better keep your tenth.

TWO *(happily):* Oh, good! Isn't that great? Why that makes me *eleven* tenths!

ONE: *Eleven* tenths? How do you figure that?

TWO: The tenth you said I could keep, plus my ten-tenths—that makes eleven.

ONE *(sighs):* You'd better come with me. We'll go where it's quiet and start again from the beginning.

TWO: Now I can buy that TV set! I'll go right down and make the deal!

(They leave.)

For Discussion

Does it bother you when the topic of discussion is giving to the church? Why?

13. Matthew and Judas

Puppets: MATTHEW and JUDAS

MATTHEW: Judas, traveling with the Master and hearing his

words, I wonder how I ever could have been a tax gatherer.

JUDAS: At least you had money of your own then.

MATTHEW: But, Judas, money isn't everything.

JUDAS: That's always said by people who don't have any. To succeed in this world, two things are needed: money and power.

MATTHEW: Jesus has no money.

JUDAS: He has *power.* If he'll just use it right.

MATTHEW: I thought that's what he does—uses it *right.*

JUDAS: Just you wait and see. One of these days we'll all live well: houses, clothes, influence.

MATTHEW: Oh no, Judas! That's not Jesus' way.

JUDAS: I can see myself with money, in a great hall, surrounded by men of influence and power. Just you wait and see!

(MATTHEW *and* JUDAS *leave.)*

For Discussion

What do you want from life? Is yours a worthy goal?

14. At the Inn

Puppets: the LANDLORD, REPORTER, PORTER, MAID

(REPORTER *enters at one side and* LANDLORD *the other.)*

LANDLORD: May I help you?

REPORTER: I'm a reporter with the *Bethlehem Star Gazette.* Someone phoned in that a story was developing out here at the motel.

LANDLORD: Story? If you mean a murder, certainly not! This is a respectable motel.

REPORTER: Are you sure nothing out of the ordinary has happened?

LANDLORD: I am. You have been misinformed.

REPORTER: May I talk to your help?

(PORTER *enters.*)

LANDLORD: They can't tell you any more than I can. Ask Fred here.

(LANDLORD *leaves.*)

REPORTER: Fred, what is your job around here?

PORTER: I'm the porter. Just call me a general flunky!

REPORTER: Do you mind answering a question or two?

PORTER: I guess not.

REPORTER: The *Bethlehem Star Gazette* got a tip a story was brewing here. Do you know anything about it?

PORTER: Story? No, Sir. Ain't been no trouble as far as I know.

REPORTER: No unusual guests?

PORTER: Nope. 'Course we're full up, what with the new census. Some o' the guests is good tippers. Some ain't. None of 'em is movie stars or nothin' like that.

REPORTER: No trouble last night?

(A MAID *passes behind them, carrying towels.)*

PORTER: None I heard of. Maggie, wait a minute. Maggie's the maid around here. Listen, Maggie, this feller's a reporter. He's asking if anything happened here last night.

MAID: Well, we run out of towels, what with everything being full. I'm just getting some around.

REPORTER: Our tipster seemed certain something unusual was going on out here. Are you sure?

MAID: Mister, outside of a baby being born in the garage . . . .

PORTER: Garage? What were people doing in the garage?

MAID: Well, old man Hopkins rented it to some migrants to stay in.

PORTER: He did?

MAID: Yeah. They had their own blankets and stuff. He just provided shelter.

PORTER: He *did?* I guess I misjudged him.

MAID: No, you didn't. The woman was about to have the baby, and they couldn't go any farther. Hopkins charged them the same as a room!

PORTER: The old skinflint!

REPORTER: That's all that happened?

MAID: Well, some truckers came by to see the baby. Musta got the news on their CB's.

REPORTER: Then I suppose our tip was wrong. A baby born in a garage isn't much of a story. I'll go back and tell my editor it was a bum steer.

(REPORTER *leaves.)*

PORTER *(calls after):* Sorry! *(to maid)* What's he expect to happen at this motel?

MAID *(laughs):* A visit from royalty, no doubt!

(PORTER *and* MAID *leave laughing.)*

For Discussion

A human failing is not to recognize the *worth* of events around us until long after they happen. How does this fit into our spiritual lives?

15. Mary and Martha

Puppets: MARY and MARTHA

MARY: Jesus is coming again! Simon says he'll be here tonight!

MARTHA: Mary, I'm as happy as you are that he's coming. But I want some help from you this time.

MARY: I help.

MARTHA: Not as much as you should. It's a lot of work caring for all those men with Jesus.

MARY: But, Martha, I hate to miss a word Jesus says. I just want to drop everything and listen to him.

MARTHA: Mary, Jesus will be in this house many times in years to come. He's young yet. You'll have plenty of time to listen to him. Come along now.

(MARY and MARTHA leave.)

For Discussion

If today were all you had left of life, what would you want to do with it? Do we know when will be the last day?

16. Philemon and Onesimus

Puppets: ONESIMUS, a runaway slave; PHILEMON, the master

ONESIMUS (bowing low): Master, forgive me!

39

PHILEMON *(surprised to see him):* Onesimus! My runaway slave! I should have you flogged, you know. Or worse.

ONESIMUS *(humbly):* Yes, Master.

PHILEMON: But I won't.

ONESIMUS: Oh, thank you, Master!

PHILEMON: I've had a letter from my friend Paul.

ONESIMUS: Your runaway slave did not run very far. The magistrates caught me. I met Paul in prison.

PHILEMON: He asks me to forgive you, Onesimus.

ONESIMUS: At first I hated Paul. Now I am a follower of Jesus the Messiah. The same Jesus you follow, Master.

PHILEMON: That's what Paul says. I have been praying about it. At first it was hard. But now—instead of punishing you, I will set you free.

ONESIMUS: I don't deserve it—but, thank you, Master.

PHILEMON: Not *master.* Paul says you are my brother, as he is my brother.

ONESIMUS *(emotionally):* Thank you, Master!

PHILEMON: *Not* master! Just—Philemon.

ONESIMUS: *Brother* Philemon, then.

PHILEMON *(wryly):* Brother. That's still going to take some getting used to!

(PHILEMON *and* ONESIMUS *leave.)*

For Discussion

After you come to accept Jesus, is it still hard to accept new attitudes and new behavior patterns, even when you know they are right? Why?

17. Caleb and Joshua

Puppets: CALEB and JOSHUA

CALEB: Why won't the people believe us? We *could* take the country! I know we could with God's help!

JOSHUA: In this case, the majority rules. We've been outvoted. Moses gave in to the report of the others.

CALEB: Why won't Moses believe us instead of them?

JOSHUA: Perhaps because he's old and tired. He has no stomach for war.

CALEB: Neither have I if the truth were known. But in my judgment we must go in, Joshua.

JOSHUA: We shall, Caleb. One day we shall.

(CALEB *and* JOSHUA *leave.*)

For Discussion
1. Does fear ever stop you from doing what you know is right and wise?
2. When you follow a wrong course, do you spend endless time in regret?
3. Is this wise?

18. Abraham and Lot

Puppets: ABRAHAM and LOT

ABRAHAM: I'm sorry our people cannot get along. It is better we separate. Nephew, you have the choice of the land.

LOT: Thank you, Uncle.

ABRAHAM: Over here is Canaan. It is a rugged and difficult land. Over there is the fertile plain near the cities. Which do you choose?

LOT: Do you mean it? I can choose? I take the fertile plain, of course! The cities will be handy for shopping.

ABRAHAM: I don't want you to make a mistake.

LOT: Mistake to choose the best land? Uncle, this is the greatest thing you've ever done for me.

ABRAHAM: Time will tell. *(He leaves.)*

LOT: Uncle Abraham's age is showing. Imagine giving away all that fertile land! Poor old Abraham! *(He leaves.)*

19. Pharaoh and His Steward

Puppets: PHARAOH and his STEWARD

(PHARAOH *enters, followed by his* STEWARD.)

STEWARD: O Mighty Pharaoh, the Prince Moses waits to see you. He has a—a person with him.

PHARAOH *(angrily):* Don't call him prince any more! He is a *Hebrew,* one of the slave race! That *person* is his brother, a Hebrew slave! Never call him prince again!

STEWARD *(frightened):* Yes, Sire! He—he said he must see you. He said to tell you it's a matter of life and death.

PHARAOH: As a boy, Moses always exaggerated. He's lucky it wasn't *his* death when he came back.

STEWARD: But, Sire, he said you will regret not seeing him *at once.*

PHARAOH: Another magician's trick? *(laughs)* His mind is affected. After all, what can *he* do against me, the mightiest power in the world? No, no. Tell him to go away!

(PHARAOH *and his* STEWARD *leave.*)

For Discussion

Do you ever become willful and think you don't need God's help? that you can manage on your own?

20. Square

Three puppets: GRANDPA; his grandson HANK, the reporter; and the OLD CODGER.

(The OLD CODGER *is in a rocking chair at one side. Make this of cardboard and fasten to the puppet so that the puppeteer's arm goes up through the chair.* GRANDPA *and* HANK *enter other side.)*

GRANDPA: What's on your mind, Hank?

HANK: Grandpa, I like being a reporter but sometimes I feel sorry for the people I have to write about. Some of them are so limited, so square.

GRANDPA: Being square is pretty good, Hank. Fewer squares end up on a psychiatrist's couch than the free livers.

HANK *(scoffing):* Oh, Grandpa! You don't know that for a fact.

GRANDPA *(unabashed):* I know lots of squares and not one of them has gone to a psychiatrist. So it must be good to be a square.

HANK: I don't believe it. Now, this old codger, whose story I have to write, he's going to be 100 Tuesday. Who cares?

GRANDPA: Probably he does.

HANK: But just to be 100? What's that? What has he had out of the 100 years to make him happy or his life worth living?

GRANDPA: Why not ask him?

(GRANDPA *steps aside to watch as Hank goes to* OLD CODGER.)

HANK: Sir!

OLD CODGER *(deafly)*: Eh?

HANK: Sir, can you hear me?

OLD CODGER: You ain't said nothing yet.

HANK: Sir, I'm a reporter. I want to interview you for Tuesday's paper. Will you answer some questions?

OLD CODGER: Fire away, Sonny.

HANK: You'll be 100 years old. Did you ever think you'd live to be this old?

OLD CODGER: Don't see why not. Weren't no trouble.

HANK: To what do you attribute your great age?

OLD CODGER: Survival, Sonny.

HANK: Well, yes. But how did you survive?

OLD CODGER: One day at a time. Only way to do it. That's all the good Lord gives us—one day at a time.

HANK: What I mean is, did you follow a special diet? Did you have any bad habits?

OLD CODGER: No special diet. Just whatever there was to eat. Bad habits? If you mean smokin' and drinkin'—never saw no sense in either. Better use for my money.

HANK: What about girls?

OLD CODGER: Courted one girl. Back in the hills weren't much

44

choice. She seemed likely. We was married when she hit sixteen. She up and died on me ten years ago.

HANK: I'm sorry.

OLD CODGER: What for? We had sixty-four years together. Seems fair.

HANK: Was she the only woman in your life?

OLD CODGER: If I take your meaning—and I think I do— you askin' if I fooled around?

HANK (surprised at the phrase): Well—yes, Sir. Most people do, don't they?

OLD CODGER: They do?

HANK: That's the way it seems to me.

OLD CODGER: 'Tain't no wonder, the way things is. I recollect when we come out of the hills, that war they called World War I was just ended. My, did things bust out! And they kept on bustin'. Ain't never stopped. All down hill, to my way of thinkin'. Young feller, they's too much attention goes to sex, if you'll pardon the word.

HANK: Oh?

OLD CODGER: Sex sells cars, shoes, hardware, fertilizer, and everything else. On billboards, TV, and all the printed stuff. Downright wicked. Silly, too, and misleading.

HANK: Sex is important.

OLD CODGER: Anything the good Lord made is important. But not the most important, even if the advertising men do try to make you think it is. Why, when you set sail on the ship of matrimony today, you already got your return ticket in hand!

HANK: Modern people don't believe that marriage has to be forever if the husband and wife aren't happy.

OLD CODGER: Nonsense. Nothing is always *happy*. They's ups and downs, just like the stock market. You sell off every time they's a down and you soon ain't got nothin' left. Same with marriage.

HANK: Don't tell me you never in all those sixty-four years didn't want to stray!

OLD CODGER: 'Course I won't say that! But I knowed Ellie wouldn't of stood for no nonsense! She'd a crowned me with a iron frying pan!

HANK: Were you afraid she'd leave you if you strayed?

OLD CODGER: Not Ellie. She took me for better or worse. She'd a figgered that was a *worse* and would of got us through it somehow.

HANK: I don't think many modern women would do that. None I've seen anyway.

OLD CODGER: Sure they would, Son. You just ain't looked in the right places. They's still decent, moral, honest, high-minded women around. And men, too. The other kind is what you hear about. You folks at the paper think they's more excitin'.

HANK: Do you regret anything in your life?

OLD CODGER: Jist one. The rest—well, the good Lord forgave me, and I follered suit and forgave myself.

HANK: What was the one thing you regret?

OLD CODGER: Ellie's dying off on me. I miss her. Catch myself wantin' to tell her something funny I seen. Ellie was a great one for laughin'.

HANK: Well, thank you, Sir. I hope you have a happy birthday Tuesday.

OLD CODGER: Thank you, Son.

(HANK *moves back to* GRANDPA.)

GRANDPA: How did it go?

HANK: OK, I guess. Poor old guy. He's just waiting to die, and he's done nothing in his whole life!

GRANDPA: Depends on what you want in the first place.

HANK: Grandpa, how can you be so square?

GRANDPA: Well, Hank, in this day and age it isn't easy. What it takes is real guts!

(All leave.)

For Discussion

1. Give some reasons why divorce is so prevalent.
2. Are there unnecessary divorces?
3. Decency, faithfulness, endurance, and other so-called attributes of marriage are under attack today from every quarter. What chance does your marriage have today?
4. Do you know some people who have been married thirty years or more? Ask why they have not divorced.
5. Do you think you have the stamina to make a marriage last?
6. When is the best time to avert divorce?

21. David and Goliath

Puppets: DAVID, GOLIATH, KING SAUL, ELIAB (David's oldest brother)
Props: small bundle, slingshot

(DAVID appears with small bundle. Then ELIAB enters.)

ELIAB: David! Is it really you, little brother? *(They touch.)*

DAVID: I've brought you some food from home, Eliab. *(bundle is put off stage)*

ELIAB: Thank you. We appreciate it. How is our father and the others at home?

DAVID: All well. But we miss you brothers. We thought this war would be over by now. As I came along, I saw the big army of King Saul. Victory looks sure.

ELIAB *(gloomily):* Far from sure, little brother.

DAVID *(surprised):* Why?

(GOLIATH *appears at one side. He was more than eleven feet tall, so make him much larger than the other puppets. He shouts in a deep, loud voice.*)

GOLIATH: You dogs of Israel!

ELIAB (*shaking in fear*): That's the reason why! *Goliath!*

GOLIATH (*roaring*): Why don't you come out and fight? You know we Philistines are better than you! We will conquer you!

DAVID (*awed*): He's so *big!*

ELIAB: You can say that again.

DAVID: He's so *big!*

GOLIATH: We Philistines are good sports. Also we don't like to see good men die for nothing. King Saul! Where are you?

SAUL: H-here. H-here I am, Goliath!

GOLIATH: King Saul, send out your best warrior to fight *me!* Whoever wins, the victory is to his people! Now what could be fairer? Where is your hero?

SAUL: L—let us talk it over among ourselves, Goliath!

GOLIATH: OK! I'll be back soon. (*He leaves.*)

SAUL (*grieving*): Woe is me! I have no giant to go against such a one as Goliath!

DAVID (*stoutly*): You have Eliab here!

ELIAB (*quaking*): David! Little boys should be seen and not heard.

SAUL: Eliab?

ELIAB: O King, I am no match for Goliath!

SAUL (*in despair*): Yes, you're right. He would crush you with one blow. Alas, I have no one to send out.

DAVID (*dismayed*): In the whole army? Not one?

SAUL: No, not one. Woe is me!

DAVID (*resolutely*): Then I will go!

SAUL: What? (*begins laughing*) Ha, ha, ha!

DAVID: Yes, me. You don't have anyone else, do you?

SAUL: No.

DAVID: Then I will go.

SAUL: Don't be foolish!

DAVID: I'm *not* foolish. I know with God's help I can defeat Goliath! I *can!*

SAUL: Ridiculous!

DAVID: It's not ridiculous. Are you *afraid?*

SAUL *(angrily):* So be it! Eliab, take this stubborn fool and fit him with my armor!

(DAVID *and* ELIAB *leave.)*

SAUL: His brain must be affected! Maybe it is as well his life ends here before he does harm to someone. His poor father will grieve, as well as his brothers. But if Goliath has his way, all Israel will mourn for her sons. Maybe David's foolish sacrifice will give us some time.

(ELIAB *returns with* DAVID, *who is carrying a slingshot.)*

SAUL: What's this? Where's the armor and the sword?

ELIAB *(apologetically):* They were too big and heavy for him, O King. He couldn't walk with them.

SAUL: Then where is your weapon?

DAVID: This slingshot.

SAUL *(sadly):* Child, I'm not angry with you now. I cannot let you sacrifice yourself this way after all. Can't you see it is foolish?

DAVID *(confidently):* Don't worry. I'll be OK.

SAUL: Who says so?

DAVID: God says so. Besides, it's too late. Here comes Goliath.

(GOLIATH *appears at one side.)*

GOLIATH *(roaring):* You dogs of Israel! Where is your hero to come against me?

(DAVID *moves toward* GOLIATH. ELIAB *and* SAUL *back off.)*

DAVID: Here I am, Goliath!

GOLIATH *(laughs):* Ho, ho, ho! You make a joke? I like a good laugh too. Now, where's your hero? Goliath is getting impatient!

DAVID: I'm the only hero around. I've come to fight you, Goliath, by the strength of the Lord!

GOLIATH *(roaring):* You dare make fun of Goliath? I will crush you like a bug!

DAVID *(as* GOLIATH *moves toward him):* Oh, no, you won't!

(DAVID *swings the slingshot.* GOLIATH *falls back.)*

GOLIATH: Ohhh! I am hit! I am *dead! (He rolls out of sight. Background cheers)*

ELIAB *(coming to* DAVID): I don't believe it! You did it!

DAVID: Not I. *God.* I told you so.

SAUL *(amazed):* Who are you, boy?

DAVID: Eliab is my brother. Our father is Jesse.

SAUL: From now on you shall live in the palace with me!

DAVID: As you wish. Eliab, tell Father, please.

(DAVID *and* SAUL *leave.)*

ELIAB: I go home and tell Father his little boy killed a *giant* with a little rock—and has gone to live at the *palace?* He'll think I've flipped! *(He leaves.)*

22. Do as I Say and Not . . .

These three brief skits may be done together or separately.

Puppets: DAD, SON, MOTHER, DAUGHTER, and either a dog puppet or stuffed toy dog.

(DAD *enters followed by* SON.)

SON: Dad? Are you busy?

DAD: Not especially. Just waiting for the news on TV.

SON: Can I talk to you?

DAD: Son, anytime you want to talk to your old dad, I'm ready to listen. What is it?

SON: Mary Sue accused me of cheating.

DAD: *Cheating?* Mary Sue always impressed me as a nice sensible girl. You must have provoked her. What did you do?

SON: Well, I couldn't get my math homework. Bill let me copy his. Mary Sue said that's cheating. Bill just gave me a helping hand! How is that cheating? What's cheating anyway?

DAD: Cheating is obtaining something by fraud or lying.

SON: Then I didn't cheat! Bill *gave* me the answers!

DAD: That's the wrong way to think. You did cheat someone. You cheated yourself. The teacher gave you the homework to help *you* learn math. So what you did was dishonest. You cheated Bill, too.

SON: I don't understand.

DAD: You took something without paying for it. Bill's brains and work.

SON: Is that like getting money for work and not paying the taxes out of it? Like, when Mr. Hardy paid you to sell his house and you told Mother, what Uncle Sam didn't know, didn't count?

DAD: Uh—maybe you'd better go see if your Mother needs any help.

(They leave.)

Second segment

(MOTHER *and* DAUGHTER *enter.)*

MOTHER: Come with me, dear. I have something for you. Here it is—a pretty new blouse.

51

DAUGHTER: Oh, thanks, Mom! But I thought you said we couldn't afford two blouses this month and you needed one worse than I did.

MOTHER: Oh, I got mine too. It was a real stroke of luck. There I was at the sale with all those gabby women! Everyone pulling at everything. I couldn't make up my mind between two. When I got home, I found the clerk had put *both* blouses in the bag by mistake!

DAUGHTER: But, Mother, remember when the cashier at the drugstore gave me change for ten dollars instead of five? You made me give it back!

MOTHER: That's different.

DAUGHTER: Why?

MOTHER: It was *money*.

(They leave.)

Third segment

(All puppets and the dog appear, apparently riding in a car)

DAD: Here's the motel. Keep Rover out of sight. They don't allow dogs at this motel. *(They push the dog down)* I'll get the rooms.

(DAD *leaves.)*

DAUGHTER: What if Rover barks?

MOTHER: Don't *let* him! You heard your father. If he barks anyway, we'll pretend it's from outside somewhere.

SON: I can keep him quiet!

(DAD *returns.)*

DAD: All set. Adjoining rooms at the back.

MOTHER: Good. When it gets dark we'll take Rover outside for a run.

DAUGHTER: Mom, if they don't want dogs here, why do we stay? Isn't that dishonest?

MOTHER: Of course not. Rover is such a nice dog.

DAD: Rover's all right.

SON: But he's still a dog.

DAD: Why do you kids argue every time we go on a trip? Here we are: 103 and 104. And keep that dog out of sight!

(They all leave.)

23. Whose Neighbor?

Two puppets

(ONE *enters, followed by* TWO.)

TWO: Hey wait! I want to talk to you!

ONE: Hi! Sure. What is it?

TWO: It's about your neighbor.

ONE: My neighbor? Which neighbor?

TWO: Well, he's not your next-door neighbor type. He lives two blocks down in that big apartment house.

ONE: The apartment next door to *your* house?

TWO: Yeah, that's it. Right next door to me. Anyway, this old man who lives there—his name is Simpson. Oh, I get all upset when I try to talk about it! It's terrible!

ONE: I don't believe I know anyone named Simpson.

TWO: Just listen to this. The poor old man is eighty-six and he lives all alone.

ONE: Lots of old people live alone.

TWO: But this poor old man is feeble. He can't leave the apartment.

ONE: Doesn't he have kinfolk?

TWO: He has a daughter back east and a son out west.

ONE: That's good.

TWO: *Good?* What's good about it?

ONE: It's good he has children.

TWO: No, no! It's *sad.* Neither of them cares anything for the poor old man.

ONE: How do you know?

TWO: The maids that take care of some of the apartments say so. One of them was telling my wife.

ONE: Maybe they're wrong.

TWO: When his children never come to see him and never write? Disgraceful!

ONE: That's too bad.

TWO: There he is, confined to that room. His only visitors are those maids.

ONE: You'll have to admit it's kind of them.

TWO: I suppose. They bring him one meal a day from the cafeteria in the building. That's all he has to eat.

ONE: He's lucky they care about him, then.

TWO: *Lucky?* The cafeteria is closed on Sunday and that poor old man has nothing to eat between Saturday and Monday when the maids come back. It's disgraceful!

ONE: That *is* bad.

TWO: It makes me angry every time I think of it. I've a good mind to call his children if I can just get them by phone.

ONE: I thought you said they didn't care about him.

TWO: They don't. But I'm going to call them anyway! It keeps worrying me—him with nothing to eat.

ONE: There's a quicker way to solve the problem.

TWO: What's that?

ONE: *You* could take him meals on Sunday.

(They leave.)

24. Announcement Pattern

Precede the announcement of a party, camp, or retreat with this.

Puppets: WILBUR, PRUNELLA

(WILBUR *enters, yelling with excitement.*)

WILBUR: Prunella! *Prunella! PRUNELLAAAA!*

(PRUNELLA *enters calmly.*)

PRUNELLA: Stop yelling, Wilbur. What do you want?

WILBUR *(bobbing up and down eagerly):* Guess what, Prunella! There's going to be a *super party!* *(He adds the details breathlessly. He pauses, then speaks pleadingly)* Prunella . . . .

PRUNELLA: I heard you, Wilbur.

WILBUR *(pleading):* Aw, Prunella, please go with me to the party! Huh, Prunella? Huh?

PRUNELLA: No . . . good-bye, Wilbur.

WILBUR: Aw, Prunella, you've got to go with me! You can't say no! Wait, Prunella! Don't leave till you say yes!

PRUNELLA: Good-bye, Wilbur.

WILBUR *(flies into a tantrum, yells, and jumps around):* All right, Prunella! Don't you dare leave! If you do—if you do, I'll—I'll eat some *worms* and be *sick all over the place!* Do you hear me, Prunella.

PRUNELLA *(calmly):* I do. Good-bye, Wilbur.

(PRUNELLA *leaves.* WILBUR *looks after her, then slowly follows as he says—)*

WILBUR: Aw, Prunellaaaa!

25. The Employment Agency

This skit is for fun times. The female puppet is behind a desk. Perhaps she wears spectacles and speaks with an exaggerated southern accent. Behind her is a sign, "Ace Employment Agency." The male puppet has long hair, a beard, wears a bright serape or dark jacket with rhinestones, and goggles. She is at the desk when he enters. He is loud and brash.

HE: Hey, Babe!

SHE *(primly):* I beg yoah pardon?

HE: Huh? What for?

SHE *(annoyed):* Suh, did you want something?

HE: Why, sure, Man, what else?

SHE *(impatiently after a noticeable pause):* Well! What do you want?

HE: Uh—this is an employment office. Right, Babe?

SHE: The sign says so. And my name is not Babe. It's Miss Calhoun. Miss *Euphronia Calhoun!*

HE *(enthusiastically):* Right! Mine's *Va-room! (Sounds like a motor taking off.)*

SHE *(surprised):* What kind of name is that?

HE (embarrassed laugh): Heh! Heh! My real name is *Darling, Honey Darling.* My mother's idea. Can you tie that? Now if you want to call me Honey . . . .

SHE (quickly): Well—ah—Mr.—ah—Va-room, what can I do for you?

HE: Caught the beef—(sees she doesn't understand)—uh—saw the *ad*—understand?

SHE: Yes? Which ad?

HE: About that church wanting a secretary. I need a little bread. So—I'll give it a go.

SHE (hedging): Well, now, Mr.—ah—Va-room . . . .

HE: Just Va-room, Babe. Leave off the ah.

SHE: Mr—Va-room, I hardly think that job's *right* for you—

HE: Yeah? I snap off a hundred and twenty five words a minute on the keys. I can take it down as fast as you can say Peter Piper picked a peck of pickled peppers!

SHE (apologetically): Ouah pastors hardly ever say that. Besides, well, Mr. Va-room, yoah just not the *type.*

HE: What is the type?

SHE: Oh, I don't know. But I just know yoah *not.* For one thing— look at yoah hair.

HE (pleased): Yeah. That's where I got the idea!

SHE: I don't understand.

HE (eagerly): I saw your ad, Babe. I got on my wheels and zoomed out there. To that church, I mean. That was *it!*

SHE: What was it?

HE: I knew right off it had to be my thing—my bag.

SHE: You did?

HE: Yeah. Those *windows!* All the *long hairs!* See?

SHE *(resignedly)*. Mr. Va-room, I've got to have a *long talk* with you. Follow me. *(She leaves.)*

HE *(eagerly following):* Yeah! Yeah! Yeah! *(He leaves.)*

26. Never Trust a Snake

For fellowship times. The snake wears a purple hat. Voices are important. Adam sounds naive. So does Eve until she eats the fruit.

(EVE appears.)

EVE *(calling):* Adam! . . . Adam? . . . Where are you? Oh, dear, I'll bet he's out naming those old animals again. The same thing morning, noon, and night. Adam! AAAAAAdam!

(ADAM appears.)

ADAM: You called, Eve? You sound excited. I know there's nothing wrong because what could go wrong in the Garden of Eden?

EVE *(pouting):* Adam, where were you? I've been calling and calling.

ADAM: Naming the animals, of course. What else? That's my job.

EVE *(tearfully):* You care more about that old job than you do me!

ADAM *(sighs):* Women never understand. It takes a lot of thought to name an animal. For instance there's one now I can't decide. What would *you* call that big animal—the one with heavier front legs than back. He's yellow-brown with light spots and a great long neck. I was thinking "Orbusher."

EVE: No. Giraffe.

ADAM: Giraffe? Why would you call him giraffe?

EVE: Because he looks like a giraffe. Oh, Adam, stop naming animals and spend some time with me!

ADAM: With you? Doing what?

EVE: Oh, we'll think of something. You never spend much time with me.

ADAM: Eve, my work is important. Why can't women understand that a man's work is important?

EVE: *Women?* What *women?* I'm the only one there is!

ADAM *(sternly):* Eve, I must get these animals named. Now, you be a good girl and go shopping or something.

(ADAM *leaves.)*

EVE: Chauvinist! *(sighs)* Well, there he goes—old One-Track. Even if he had stayed . . . maybe when he runs out of animals—?

(SNAKE *appears and* EVE *screams.)*

EVE: Oh, go away! Shoo! Shoo! Adam! Adam!

SNAKE *(gaily):* He can't hear you!

EVE *(startled):* You—you speak?

SNAKE: Why not. *You* do. Quite charmingly, if I may say so.

EVE *(pleased):* I do?

SNAKE: Oh, yes. I've often hidden in the grass and listened. You speak much better than that other one—Adam, you called him?

EVE: Yes. Adam. But you—you're a snake! And that *hat!*

SNAKE: In more elite circles I'm called a serpent. And I like purple. It does something for me.

EVE: Serpent?

SNAKE *(enunciating clearly):* Ser—pent. See how nicely it rolls on the tongue?

EVE: I—I guess so. Why are you here?

SNAKE: Oh, my dear, I was forgetting. You are so charming. Well I've come with important news for *you.*

EVE *(intrigued):* For me? Not Adam?

SNAKE: We-e-ell, forgive me, my dear, but Adam is just a bit slow. And he does have an appalling lack of a sense of humor. How you put up with him—

EVE *(sighs):* You do understand!

SNAKE *(sympathetically):* Indeed yes. That's why I've brought *you* the news.

EVE *(excited):* What news?

SNAKE *(secretively):* Shhh! Well—you know that tree in the middle of the Garden?

EVE *(also secretively):* You mean—the one we can't touch?

SNAKE: That's it. Did you ever wonder why you were told not to touch it?

EVE: No, but it is strange, isn't it? All that delicious looking fruit. I don't think it was very logical putting it there in the first place.

SNAKE: Exactly! You are so right. The news is about that tree. *(looks about as if to spy out evesdroppers)* I have it from *very reliable sources*—close to the *TOP*, you know—

EVE *(eagerly):* Yes, yes? Go on!

SNAKE: The truth is—if you or Adam eat the fruit from *that* tree— you'll be smarter than anyone in the whole world!

EVE *(disappointed):* I'm already smarter than anyone in the whole world.

SNAKE *(annoyed):* Suffering cobras, woman! Don't you under- stand? You'll know everything there is to know!

EVE *(awed):* As much as—?

SNAKE: Of course! Why else were you warned away?

EVE *(shocked): Jealousy?*

SNAKE *(nervously):* Now I didn't say that!

EVE: I see . . . I think. But we were told that great harm would come?

SNAKE: Don't be silly. Would HE harm *you?* Oh, my dear, there are quite a few of everything else but only two of you. You're *valuable.*

EVE: That's true. Oh, let's find Adam and tell him!

SNAKE *(slyly):* Wait! You don't think he'll *believe* us, do you?

EVE *(thinking):* I—I guess not. Oh, dear, if he weren't so one-tracked!

SNAKE: I have it! You eat the fruit first. Then you can persuade Adam by your great knowledge.

EVE: That's a good idea. Why didn't I think of it?

SNAKE: You would, in time.

EVE: Thanks!

(EVE *leaves.)*

SNAKE: Well, that wasn't too hard. Flattery is like butter. It makes everything else slide down more easily. I'll leave before she comes back.

(SNAKE *leaves. Then* EVE *returns. Now her voice is low and sultry and her manner no longer naive.)*

EVE: Well, well. What do you know about that? That snake! What a sly one he is! *Now* what do I do? (ADAM *appears.)* There's Adam. I haven't noticed before—he's the best looking man in the world! He's *got* to eat that fruit. Well, here goes.

ADAM: I'm back, Eve.

EVE *(moves close to him):* Woo, woo! You sure are, Adam, baby!

ADAM *(puzzled):* Eve! What's come over you?

EVE *(nudging him):* Why nothing, darling! Touch me and see. Go on—touch me!

ADAM *(moving away):* You're different. I don't think I like you this way.

EVE *(snuggling against him):* What way, Popsy?

ADAM: This way. Whatever it is. What's happened?

EVE: Adam, I just ate some of that fruit!

ADAM *(horrified):* From the Forbidden Tree? You didn't!

EVE *(gaily):* Oh, yes, I did! But I don't want *you* to touch it, Adam, baby.

ADAM *(suspiciously):* Why not?

EVE *(lightly):* Only one of us needs to be that smart—and that's little ole me!

ADAM: What do you mean—smart?

EVE: Brace yourself, Adam, baby. That tree—the one *we* were told *not* to touch? It has the secret of all knowledge. That's why he didn't want us to eat the fruit.

ADAM: But you did?

EVE: I sure did.

ADAM *(secretively):* What's it like, Eve? How does it feel?

EVE: I can't tell you. But don't worry. I'll be smart enough for both of us.

ADAM *(sternly):* The man is the leader. The man should be smarter than the woman!

EVE *(aside):* That'll be the day!

ADAM: What was that?

EVE: I said, what did you say?

ADAM: The man should be smarter than the woman. I'm going to eat some of the fruit myself. Don't try to stop me. Anything you can do I can do better! *(He leaves.)*

EVE: That sounds like a good song title. What I need is a guitar. Someone should invent one. I can see it now. Me with a group. We could call ourselves The First Generation!

(SNAKE appears.)

SNAKE: I saw Adam near the tree.

EVE: He's gone to eat the fruit too.

SNAKE: So you persuaded him.

EVE *(innocently):* Who, me? Oh, no. Men are leaders. Adam made up his own mind.

SNAKE: That's what he thinks. My dear, you can't fool me.

EVE: I guess not. Tell me—why did you pick me?

SNAKE: Two reasons. First, who else was there? Second, the devil made me do it!

EVE: Snakey, baby, I ought to be mad at you. But I see you can't help it. After all you are a *snake!*

(EVE *leaves.)*

SNAKE: Bigot! Classifying all serpents the same. They *aren't* the same. *If* there's a moral here, it must be: Never trust a snake wearing a purple hat.

(SNAKE *leaves.)*

27. Be Glad You're You

This skit shows children, and even adults, that being your best self is the best to be.

Puppets: two, one black and one white. Each wears a funny hat. The white puppet has a feather in his hat.

(The BLACK PUPPET *enters, then the* WHITE.)

BLACK: Hey, Man!

WHITE: Hey, yourself, Man! Where you been?

BLACK: Oh, around.

WHITE: Me, too.

BLACK: Hey, Man, how about that hat?

WHITE *(pleased):* Yeah, how about it? Yours isn't too bad either. *Swave! (He mispronounces suave.)*

BLACK: Right! Where you going?

WHITE: To tell a story to some kids.

BLACK: Why for?

WHITE: Aw, my mom promised this lady over at the nursery school I would.

BLACK: What kinda story?

WHITE: Just a story.

BLACK: Tell it to me.

WHITE: Aw, you wouldn't like it.

BLACK: Practice on me. Go on.

WHITE *(reluctantly):* OK. Well, once upon a time—

BLACK: I've heard it before!

WHITE *(annoyed):* How do you know you've heard it before? I haven't even started it yet!

BLACK: You said, "once upon a time," didn't you? Well, I've heard it before.

WHITE *(disgusted):* All stories begin, "once upon a time."

BLACK: They do?

WHITE: Yes, they do! Now stop interrupting. Once upon a time there was this little girl, and her mom made her a red cape with a hood.

BLACK *(rattling off rapidly):* And they called her Little Red Riding Hood and she lived across the woods from her old granny, and one day her granny was sick and Red Riding Hood's mom said, "Now you get right over to Granny's with this nice chicken soup 'cause she's feeling poorly and—

WHITE: Wait a minute! Wait a minute!

BLACK *(paying no heed)*:—and off she skedaddled, and then in the woods she met this bad old wolf, and he said (a mincing voice) "Where you going, missy?" and she said, "To see my poor old sick granny," and the wolf looked at her and thought, "What a dish! She'd taste mighty good on a nice spring evening with 'taters and collards on the side," and then the wolf ran ahead to Granny's—

WHITE *(yelling)*: Stop! What do you think you're doing?

BLACK *(taking his first deep breath)*: Telling myself this story to see if I've heard it before. Now when the wolf got to Granny's, he pretended he was Red Riding Hood and—

WHITE *(angrily)*: If you can tell it to yourself, of course you've heard it before!

BLACK: You know, that was some stupid old lady.

WHITE: What do you mean, stupid?

BLACK: Couldn't tell the difference between her grandchild and a mean, old wolf. I'm not going to tell that story. It's silly!

WHITE: You weren't supposed to tell it in the first place. I was. Besides, this story is very, very old. You can't say it's silly.

BLACK: Just tell me—how could that wolf swallow that old lady whole?

WHITE *(irritated)*: How do I know? All I know is—he did.

BLACK: Can you prove it?

WHITE: I don't have to prove it. That's the story.

BLACK: Well, when that woodsman came along and cut that old wolf open and let that old lady out—I bet one thing!

WHITE: Yeah? What?

BLACK: I bet she was a mess?

WHITE: Well, maybe I'll tell another story. I have to tell something since I got all dressed up for it.

BLACK: Where did you get the feather?

WHITE: Like it?

BLACK: Yeah, Man. Bet no one looks like us.

WHITE: Come to think of it, we don't even look like each other.

BLACK: That's good. I'm *not* like anyone else. I'm *me*.

WHITE: And I'm me. But sometimes I'd like to look like you.

BLACK: What for?

WHITE: 'Cause if I was black, I couldn't get freckles.

BLACK: Well, if I was white, I could use eye shadow!

WHITE: What's stopping you?

BLACK: What would be the use?

WHITE: If I was black, I could stay out in the sun longer than anybody.

BLACK: If I was white, I could look pale when I got sick.

WHITE: What's the good of that?

BLACK: Get more sympathy, Man!

WHITE: Well, if I was black and I didn't wash, no one could tell.

BLACK: Wooeee! Yes, they could!

WHITE: How?

BLACK: If you didn't wash, you wouldn't smell like a rose!

WHITE: Then we might as well stay like we are.

BLACK: 'Specially since we can't do anything about it. We better get going to that nursery school.

WHITE: It's still early. Let's go get us a hamburger first.

BLACK: OK. I'll get me a hamburger with fries and a *vanilla* milk shake.

WHITE: And I'll get me a hamburger with fries and a *chocolate* milk shake!

66

BOTH *(with feeling):* Yeahhhh!

(They leave.)

28. The Stuck-up Stick Up

This skit is for fellowships or parties. The NARRATOR stands at one side.

Puppets: the BURGLAR and the STICK-UP MAN.
A prop, the wall safe, is a small carton with a simulated knob drawn on. Inside is a bottle labeled GLUE.

NARRATOR: Once upon a time there was a burglar—

BURGLAR *(pops into view):* That's me!

NARRATOR: One night he entered a house to burgle.

BURGLAR: That's what I did.

NARRATOR: Nobody was home.

BURGLAR: Of course not! I didn't see a light anywhere.

NARRATOR: So he located the wall safe.

BURGLAR: Here it is!

NARRATOR: And he opened it skillfully.

BURGLAR *(busy at safe front):* I'm one of the best.

NARRATOR: Eagerly he looked inside.

BURGLAR *(shocked and dismayed):* A gallon of *glue?* *(He pulls out the bottle so the label is seen.)* Just a gallon of *glue?* There's got to be more than this! *(He looks again—discouraged.)* That's all. A gallon of glue. *(He hears a noise.)* What's that noise? Someone's coming! *(He puts the glue back in the safe and twirls the knob.)*

(The STICK-UP MAN *enters. He has a gun.)*

STICK-UP: Stick 'em up!

BURGLAR *(terrified, shaking)* Don't s-s-shoot! I don't have a gun! You've got me. I give up. Call the police.

STICK-UP *(surprised):* The *police?* Who wants the police?

BURGLAR: Aren't you the owner?

STICK-UP *(laughs):* Owner? No! I'm here to steal what's in that safe!

BURGLAR: Be my guest.

STICK-UP: So you can't get it open, eh?

BURGLAR: Well—it's a sticky problem.

STICK-UP *(harshly):* Well, when you get it open, you're out of luck. It's all mine!

BURGLAR *(nervously):* Oh, I'm not arguing. Take it all!

STICK-UP *(suspiciously):* There's something funny going on here.

BURGLAR: I—I guess so. If you have a sense of humor.

STICK-UP *(nastily):* I *don't.* And I'm *mean!*

BURGLAR *(groans):* Ohhhhh! Then I'm in trouble!

STICK-UP: Open that safe! I might even give you a share. A small one, of course.

BURGLAR: I—I'd rather not.

STICK-UP *(harshly):* Do you want your head shot off?

BURGLAR *(quavering):* N—not particularly!

STICK-UP *(sneers):* A wise guy, huh? OK, just for that, I'm taking it all! You ain't gittin' nothin'!

BURGLAR *(quavering):* That's OK with me.

STICK-UP *(suspiciously):* I still say something funny's going on here. Move over! I'll open the safe myself. Remember! This gun is pointed at *you!*

BURGLAR: I—I see it!

STICK-UP: Don't move! I'm keeping my eyes on you!

BURGLAR: Then how can you open the safe?

STICK-UP *(puzzled):* That is a problem. It looks like you'll have to open the safe for me.

BURGLAR: But that's a crime!

STICK-UP *(roughly):* Either open the safe or I'll shoot you!

BURGLAR *(moves quickly to safe):* I—I was just going to open it! *(works at knob)* It's stuck!

STICK-UP *(pokes him with gun):* Open that safe!

BURGLAR *(opens it):* It's open!

STICK-UP: Put the stuff in this bag! *(picks up a small bag and gives to the* BURGLAR*)* Hurry!

BURGLAR *(obeying):* I'm hurrying! I'm hurrying!

STICK-UP *(taking bag):* Now you stay here for five minutes before you try to follow.

(STICK-UP MAN *leaves.* BURGLAR *looks after him a moment.)*

BURGLAR *(sighing in relief):* That's going to be one stuck-up stick up!

NARRATOR: There ought to be a moral in all this.

BURGLAR: The wages of sin is glue?

NARRATOR: Certainly not. Don't you see how useless this way of life is? Aren't you sorry? Just a little bit?

BURGLAR: I guess so. It's certainly taught me a lesson.

NARRATOR: Good! Now what's the lesson?

BURGLAR: On my next job I'll be sure the loot is worth the trouble.

(NARRATOR and BURGLAR *leave.)*

29. One Sunday Morning in Birdborough

Puppets: two BIRDS, wearing hats and costumes. Why not tape organ music and congregational singing for appropriate times in the script?

(Mrs. Oriole appears first, followed by Mrs. Jay.)

MRS. ORIOLE: Good morning, Mrs. Jay.

MRS. JAY: May I sit with you this morning?

MRS. ORIOLE: I'll move over . . . there.

MRS. JAY: Thank you.

MRS. ORIOLE: It's nothing. You usually sit with Mrs. Crow, don't you?

MRS. JAY: Yes, but never again.

MRS. ORIOLE: Oh?

MRS. JAY: Why do you say "oh" at me like that?

MRS. ORIOLE *(apologetically):* I just said "oh."

MRS. JAY *(complaining):* I may as well tell it all. Ever since I joined the Birdborough Church, I've been sitting in the same seat . . . by Mrs. Crow.

MRS. ORIOLE: I know. We all know.

MRS. JAY: So you've noticed. Well, no one else wants to sit by her. And I felt sorry for her.

MRS. ORIOLE: Oh?

MRS. JAY: Yes—"oh." But no more. Every Sunday she comes late to the worship service. Then she *crawls* over me and drops her umbrella with a clatter. Everyone turns to see who's making all the noise.

MRS. ORIOLE: If you moved over and let her have the aisle seat—

MRS. JAY *(indignantly):* Never! Let *her* get here first and take the aisle seat. *I* am here first and that's my favorite seat!

MRS. ORIOLE: Then I'm glad I moved over for you—if it's that important.

MRS. JAY: Certainly it is! There's no excuse for her to be late. Her children are grown and she lives just down the lane.

MRS. ORIOLE: Just as some people talk a lot, some people are always late.

MRS. JAY: *She* is. Well, today when she arrives, late as usual, she won't find me waiting. Oh, Oh! Look who's sitting there this morning.

MRS. ORIOLE: It's Mrs. Cardinal, isn't it?

MRS. JAY: Of course it's Mrs. Cardinal! Who else in Birdborough wears so much red! So—so *garish.*

MRS. ORIOLE: Oh?

MRS. JAY *(annoyed):* What do you mean—"oh?"

MRS. ORIOLE: I rather like red.

MRS. JAY: You can overdo things, you know. Now Mrs. Crow could do with a little color. When Mrs. Crow arrives, what a pair they'll make. Now I try to keep Mrs. Crow from talking so much in service, but everybody knows Mrs. Cardinal never shuts up. No consideration at all!

MRS. ORIOLE *(significantly):* It does disturb when people talk in the service.

MRS. JAY: Amen!

MRS. ORIOLE *(half-whispering):* The choir is coming in. We'd better be still.

(From this point Mrs. Oriole speaks in a stage whisper. Background: congregational singing)

MRS. JAY *(normal voice):* Chatter, chatter, chatter. That's all some people do. Never listen to old Brother Owl. Although I'm sure

71

he's preached last Sunday's sermon three other times at least. What did you say? I can't hear over all this singing!

MRS. ORIOLE *(softly):* Nothing.

MRS. JAY: Look at Mr. Robin. Since he's minister of music, he *should* lead congregational singing, but does he have to do it so energetically? A little dignity wouldn't hurt.

MRS. ORIOLE: Sh!

MRS. JAY: What's the special music this morning?

MRS. ORIOLE *(whispering):* Mr. Meadowlark.

MRS. JAY: Speak up! I can't hear you.

MRS. ORIOLE *(whispering louder):* Mr. Meadowlark is doing a solo.

MRS. JAY *(complaining):* Not again? He sings so loud it hurts your ears. You can't hear what anyone else is saying.

MRS. ORIOLE: You're supposed to *listen.*

MRS. JAY: He should exercise more control.

MRS. ORIOLE: Oh?

MRS. JAY: There you go again.

MRS. ORIOLE: Sh! Listen to Mr. Meadowlark.

(background: male solo)

MRS. JAY: Do you feel a draft? There go my sinuses again. Don't you feel that draft?

MRS. ORIOLE *(softly):* I'm quite comfortable.

MRS. JAY: Our deacons are incompetent! Can't even adjust the air conditioning properly.

MRS. ORIOLE *(whispering):* They can't please everyone.

MRS. JAY: That's as may be. But with my health . . . I said, with my health . . .

MRS. ORIOLE: Oh?

MRS. JAY: There you go again!

MRS. ORIOLE: Let's listen.

MRS. JAY: My dear! No one knows the front I put up . . . I say, no one knows the front I put up. My doctor says he's never seen a case like mine.

MRS. ORIOLE: Oh?

MRS. JAY: You keep saying that!

MRS. ORIOLE: Just what is wrong?

MRS. JAY: He can't quite pin it down.

MRS. ORIOLE: Sh! Brother Owl is ready to speak.

(background, man reading Scripture)

MRS. JAY: Ah, ha! There comes Mrs. Crow! Does *she* look surprised. There she goes, pushing by Mrs. Cardinal. Oh, oh. Hear her umbrella fall?

MRS. ORIOLE: Sh!

MRS. JAY: Look at them, will you? Talking away! The people around them are turning to look. I wouldn't be that thoughtless for anything!

MRS. ORIOLE: Oh?

(MRS. ORIOLE *and* MRS. JAY *leave.*)

30. The News Today

This skit deals with a familiar Bible story as if it were in TV news today. Use for fellowships, of course, but it might be done for a Bible class—a fresh approach. At one side of the playing area is the news desk with a mike. Use the other side for interviews.

Puppets: ANCHOR MAN, HAROLD SHINBONE (the international reporter), LON LOOSESITTER (the domestic reporter), PROTESTER, MADGE MINION (the ecology reporter), SWATS HARDER (the sports reporter), SPECTATOR, NOAH, HANNAH (his wife), SUNNY SHADE (the weather person), and five assorted ANIMALS, either stuffed or puppets.

(ANCHOR MAN *appears behind desk.*)

ANCHOR: Good evening, ladies and gentlemen. This is the six o'clock news from Channel 2, Halter Highkite reporting. In the news tonight is a report on ecology, latest sports and weather, the international and domestic scene, and a special about an unusual local enterprise. First the international scene. Harold Shinbone reporting.

(HAROLD SHINBONE *appears at other side.*)

HAROLD: This week, his Majesty the king is entertaining the delegates from the province. At a state dinner, lasting three days, the king presented jeweled amulets to each delegate. This was his way of thanking the delegates for the beautiful maidens presented to him during the first course by the delegates. This state occasion was marred by an untimely incident. During the festivities one of the maidens fell or was pushed from the palace roof and soon died. Her body was found by forty slaves bringing trays of roast peacock and other succulent foods from the palace kitchens to the banquet hall. The delegate, whose gift she was, announced that a replacement will arrive by the next caravan. Harold Shinbone reporting from the palace.

(HAROLD *leaves.*)

ANCHOR: Thank you, Harold. On the domestic scene we hear from Lon Loosesitter.

(LON LOOSESITTER *appears.*)

LON: Palace guards were called out to assist city police when a protest march in the business district threatened to disrupt trade. I have with me one of the protesters. (PROTESTER *joins him, still carrying small sign.*) Mr. Agin, what is your group protesting?

PROTESTER: Bread!

LON: You are against *bread?*

PROTESTER: Nosirree! Against not having it! We want bread!

LON: Why don't you have bread?

PROTESTER: No wheat coming into the port, that's why.

LON: I see ships coming into port. Why no wheat?

PROTESTER: Because of all the folderol that's coming in those ships! No room for wheat.

LON: Folderol?

PROTESTER: Humming bird's tongues, spices from the East, young girls from the provinces, and such like. All for the king's crowd. None of it for us. We're just common people. We don't ask for one of those maidens. Although . . . well, we'll be satisfied with bread—rye, pumpernickel, thin sliced—any kind we can get.

LON: I see. Well, thank you, Mr. Agin. Good luck! (PROTESTER *leaves.)* This is another incident which shows the unrest among the people. These protests are coming more often and are more violent every day. This is Lon Loosesitter at the scene.

(LON *leaves.)*

ANCHOR: We have a special report on the nation's ecology. Let's hear from Madge Minion in the field.

(MADGE MINION *appears. Behind her from time to time various* ANIMALS *pop up. Her report begins calmly and grows more and more hysterical.)*

MADGE: A strange phenomenon is occurring. (ANIMAL *comes up and nudges her)* Ooops! As you see, animals are coming into the country. *(another* ANIMAL *nudges)* Ouch! Animals not ordinarily seen in this area. Animal experts are unable to account for the strange invasion. They travel in groups. *(third* ANIMAL *comes up and nudges)* Look out! As I said, they travel in groups not usually compatible. I just saw some big-horn sheep moving along peacefully in a pack of big cats: lions, cheetahs, and jackals.

(fourth ANIMAL *up)* Oooh! They pay no attention to other animals or people along their way. They are heading for the desert. The problem created, according to Dr. Heepo Brains—the problem is—the problem is the great number of new animals. *(a fifth* ANIMAL, *they crowd* MADGE) Ohhhhh! The animals native to this area—area, that is—will be disrupted—please excuse me!—will be deprived of their rights. A committee—committee headed by Dr. Bevans—correction—Dr. Brains—appointed by the in—institute—is—is—Oh, dear!—is investigating. Go away! Go away! Scat! This is Madge Minion—Ohhhhh!

(MADGE *and* ANIMALS *disappear.*)

ANCHOR: Madge! Madge? Well, anyway thank you for that report. Now for sports. Come in, Swats Harder!

(SWATS *enters.*)

SWATS: A quiet day on the sports scene. The only game in the Mediterranean League ended in a tie between Sodom and Gomorrah. The game was called because of darkness. The tie will be played off after the regular season ends. No games in the Euphrates League today. Tyre was the scene of galley races this afternoon. The winning galley, belonging to the king, of course, reached the unprecedented speed of thirty slaves an hour. Nubians will be brought in to reman the oars for next week's race. In the provinces, bearbaiting is a coming popular sport, attracting large crowds of spectators. This reporter visited one of the contests this week and talked to a typical spectator. (SPECTATOR *enters.*) Sir, I see you just attended the bearbaiting contest.

SPECTATOR: Wowee!

SWATS: I gather you liked what you saw?

SPECTATOR: Wowee! The greatest! Beats watching a state execution.

SWATS: You attend those also?

SPECTATOR: Doesn't everybody? Let the suckers have it, I say. Shouldn'ta got caught.

SWATS: This contest today—how would you rate it?

SPECTATOR: Well, on a scale of zero to ten, about five. Now, last month, over in Sidon, I saw the greatest match of all! That dog and that bear were as evenly matched as you can get! That's what makes a good fight. Neither would give up until both were bloody pulps. Wowee! What a contest!

SWATS: Do you believe these contests are a new sports trend?

SPECTATOR: Sure. Why not?

(SPECTATOR *leaves.*)

SWATS: This concludes the sports report. This is Swats Harder.

(SWATS *leaves.*)

ANCHOR: Thank you, Swats. Now we come to our special feature. In the Channel 2 news last week there was an item about the man in the nearby desert who is building a boat. We felt our viewers might like to meet this ambitious builder. We welcome Mr. Noah and his wife, Hannah. (NOAH *and* HANNAH *enter.*) Mr. Noah, Mrs. Noah, welcome to Channel 2. Now, Mr. Noah, our reporters tell us you are building a boat out there in the desert.

NOAH: 'Tain't exactly *desert.* It's our *farm.* Ain't it. Mother?

HANNAH: Yes, Noah.

ANCHOR: Well, that doesn't matter.

NOAH: It does to us, Mister! You know how hard it is to make a go of it in that desert?

HANNAH: Now, Father!

ANCHOR: I'm sure you do a good job. Now, back to the boat. Is it real?

NOAH: If it ain't, we all gotta learn to swim.

ANCHOR: I don't understand, Mr. Noah. What possessed you to build a boat where there's no water?

NOAH: There will be, young feller. Just you wait and see.

ANCHOR: On what do you base that statement.

NOAH: On the good Lord, that's who. He said, build a boat 'cause it's gonna rain forty days and forty nights. Water's gonna fill this here town and our farm and everywhere. Clear over the mountaintops.

ANCHOR *(amused):* When is this *alleged* deluge to occur?

NOAH *(reprovingly):* I don't know, young feller. But when Jehovah God says "Build!" I reckon he knows what he's talking about. So I build.

HANNAH: Father—*we* build. Don't forget the boys and us women too.

NOAH: OK, Mother.

ANCHOR: Boys? You have sons who helped in this enterprise?

NOAH: The boys helped build the boat if I take your meaning. Yep, three boys. All married to mighty fine girls.

ANCHOR: If we'd known, we would have included your sons in this interview.

NOAH: Can't. They're out gittin' in the animals.

ANCHOR: Animals?

NOAH: We're loadin' up that boat with at least two of every kind. Male and female if you excuse me saying. Seven of the clean animals.

ANCHOR *(astonished):* I haven't seen this boat. Are you telling me it's large enough to contain all those animals?

NOAH: Sure. And all us folks too. What did you think we wuz buildin'? A skiff?

ANCHOR: No, but—but—why, that must be larger than the palace of the king!

NOAH: It better be or we're gonna be mighty crowded. It's a fine ark. Had a good shipwright—the good Lord himself. We just followed orders.

ANCHOR: Now about those animals—

NOAH: All I got to say is this whole thing better git goin'! Them animals could git to be quite a problem.

HANNAH: That's right, Father. Whose problem? Why me and the girls, of course. Ain't nothing prideful about cleanin' up after animals.

ANCHOR: What will you do with all those animals if you have miscalculated?

NOAH: I ain't "mis" nothin', young feller. We're taking the Lord at his word. Now me and the missus have to get on home. Too bad we won't see you no more. Considerin' your upbringing, you been mighty kind to Mother and me. Good-bye. Come, Mother.

(NOAH *and* HANNAH *leave.*)

ANCHOR: Poor old fellow. Really a sad case. We'll try to arrange a follow up in a couple of weeks. Meanwhile the authorities need to be mindful of all those animals out there. Now, to our weather person, Sunny Shade.

(SUNNY SHADE, *a female, appears.*)

SUNNY: Good evening. On the weather map, radar picks up rain showers west of us. At the moment these are scattered. However with the high pressure we mentioned in yesterday's report and the new low moving in from the coast, the possibility of some rain in your area seems good. Tomorrow look for a low of seventy-five and a high in the mid-nineties. Twenty percent chance of light showers. Take an umbrella with you to the office in the morning. No change indicated for the remainder of the week. Listen to the ten o'clock weather forecast for further details. This is your weather person, Sunny Shade.

(SUNNY *leaves.*)

ANCHOR: This concludes the six o'clock news from Channel 2. For later developments, tune in at ten tonight and seven in the morning. Halter Highkite bidding you good evening. *(He leaves.)*